# DONKEY GOSPEL

**WINNER OF THE 1997
JAMES LAUGHLIN AWARD
OF THE ACADEMY OF AMERICAN POETS**

The James Laughlin Award is given to
commend and support a poet's second book.
The only award of its kind in the United
States, it is named in honor of the poet and
publisher James Laughlin, who founded New
Directions in 1936. The award is endowed by
a gift to The Academy of American Poets
from the Drue Heinz Trust.

**JUDGES FOR 1997**
*Yusef Komunyakaa*
*Heather McHugh*
*William Matthews*

# DONKEY GOSPEL

*Tony Hoagland*

POEMS

Graywolf Press

Publication of this volume is made possible
in part by a grant provided by the Minnesota
State Arts Board through an appropriation
by the Minnesota State Legislature, and
by a grant from the National Endowment
for the Arts. Significant support has also
been provided by Dayton's, Mervyn's, and
Target stores through the Dayton Hudson
Foundation, the Andrew W. Mellon
Foundation, the McKnight Foundation,
the General Mills Foundation, the St. Paul
Companies, and other generous contributions
from foundations, corporations, and
individuals. To these organizations and
individuals we offer our heartfelt thanks.

Published by Graywolf Press
250 Third Avenue North, Suite 600
Minneapolis, Minnesota 55401
All rights reserved.

www.graywolfpress.org

Published in the United States of America

ISBN 978-1-55597-268-4 (paperback)
ISBN 978-1-55597-276-9 (limited edition, cloth)

11  12  13  14  15  16  17  18

Library of Congress Catalog Card Number:
97-80081

Cover art: Roger Brown,
"Ventura Freeway Landscaped," 1993.
Courtesy Phyllis Kind Gallery,
Chicago/New York.
Photographed by William H. Bengston.

Cover design: Jeenee Lee Design

## ACKNOWLEDGMENTS

Many thanks to the journals in which
the poems below previously appeared:

*AGNI*: Beauty, Just Spring
*American Poetry Review*: Cry Me a River
*Arizona Quarterly*: Here in Berkeley
*Black Warrior Review*: Fred Had Watched a Lot of *Kung Fu* Episodes,
    Honda Pavarotti
*Denver Quarterly*: Arrows
*The Gettysburg Review*: Game, Auden
*Harvard Review*: Lie Down with a Man, Mission
*Indiana Review*: Mistaken Identity
*The Massachusetts Review*: Are You Experienced?, Ecology
*New England Review*: Medicine, The Replacement
*North American Review*: The Confessional Mode
*Orion Magazine*: From This Height
*Passages North*: Lucky, Totally
*Ploughshares*: Jet, Self-Improvement, Lawrence
*Puerto Del Sol*: Muy Macho, Reading *Moby-Dick* at 30,000 Feet, Brave World,
    Dickhead
*The Quotable Moose*: Totally
*Third Coast*: Hearings
*The Threepenny Review*: Candlelight, Benevolence
*TriQuarterly*: Adam and Eve, Memory As a Hearing Aid,
    Why We Went and What We Found

A grant from the National Endowment from the Arts made the writing
of these poems possible; likewise, I am very grateful for several visits
to Yaddo art colony. Also, thanks to Emerson College and *Ploughshares*
for their generous Zacharis Prize.

And the community of poetry and friendship which is indispensable to
my life: JoAnn Beard, Bruce Cohen, Carl Dennis, Richard McCann,
David Rivard, Mary Ruefle, Betty Sasaki, Gibb Windahl, Dean Young,
and the Warren Wilson Community.

In particular, two parties helped with these poems: Marie Howe,
invaluable friend and co-thinker; and my writing group in Maine, Los
Bachelores Perdidos: Louis Sinclair, Bruce Spang, and Peter Harris.

# DONKEY GOSPEL

*for*
*Peter Harris*
*and*
*Steve Orlen*

# DONKEY GOSPEL

We are clouds,
and terrible things happen in clouds
DEAN YOUNG

You ask me to sing a sad song
How motherfucker can I sing a sad song
when I remember Zion?
JACK SPICER

# Jet

Sometimes I wish I were still out
on the back porch, drinking jet fuel
with the boys, getting louder and louder
as the empty cans drop out of our paws
like booster rockets falling back to Earth

and we soar up into the summer stars.
Summer. The big sky river rushes overhead,
bearing asteroids and mist, blind fish
and old space suits with skeletons inside.
On Earth, men celebrate their hairiness,

and it is good, a way of letting life
out of the box, uncapping the bottle
to let the effervescence gush
through the narrow, usually constricted neck.

And now the crickets plug in their appliances
in unison, and then the fireflies flash
dots and dashes in the grass, like punctuation
for the labyrinthine, untrue tales of sex
someone is telling in the dark, though

no one really hears. We gaze into the night
as if remembering the bright unbroken planet
we once came from,
to which we will never
be permitted to return.
We are amazed how hurt we are.
We would give anything for what we have.

# Mistaken Identity

I thought I saw my mother
in the lesbian bar,
with a salt gray crew cut, a nose stud
and a tattoo of a parrot on her arm.
She was sitting at a corner table,
leaning forward to ignite, on someone's match,
one of those low-tar things she used to smoke,

and she looked happy to be alive again
after her long marriage
to other people's needs,
her twenty-year stint as Sisyphus,
struggling to push
a blue Ford station wagon full of screaming kids
up a moutainside of groceries.

My friend Debra had brought me there
to educate me on the issue
of my own unnecessariness,
and I stood against the wall,  trying to look
simultaneously nonviolent

and  nonchalant, watching couples
slowdance in the  female dark,
but feeling speechless,  really,
as the first horse to meet the first
horseless carriage on a cobbled street.

That's when I noticed Mom,
whispering into the delicate
seashell ear of a brunette,
running  a fingertip along
the shoreline of a tank top,

as if death had taught her finally
not to question what she wanted
and not to hesitate
in reaching out and taking it.

I want to figure out everything
right now, before I die,
but I admit that in the dark
(where a whole life can be mistaken) cavern of that bar
it took me one, maybe two big minutes

to find my footing
and to aim my antiquated glance
over the shoulder of that woman
pretending not to be my mother,
as if I were looking for someone else.

# Reading *Moby-Dick* at 30,000 Feet

At this height, Kansas
is just a concept,
a checkerboard design of wheat and corn

no larger than the foldout section
of my neighbor's travel magazine.
At this stage of the journey

I would estimate the distance
between myself and my own feelings
is roughly the same as the mileage

from Seattle to New York,
so I can lean back into the upholstered interval
between Muzak and lunch,

a little bored, a little old and strange.
I remember, as a dreamy
backyard kind of kid,

tilting up my head to watch
those planes engrave the sky
in lines so steady and so straight

they implied the enormous concentration
of good men,
but now my eyes flicker

from the in-flight movie
to the stewardess's pantyline,
then back into my book,

where men throw harpoons at something
much bigger and probably
better than themselves,

wanting to kill it, wanting
to see great clouds of blood erupt
to prove that they exist.

Imagine being born and growing up,
rushing through the world for sixty years
at unimaginable speeds.

Imagine a century like a room so large,
a corridor so long
you could travel for a lifetime

and never find the door,
until you had forgotten
that such a thing as doors exist.

Better to be on board the *Pequod*,
with a mad one-legged captain
living for revenge.

Better to feel the salt wind
spitting in your face,
to hold your sharpened weapon high,

to see the glisten
of the beast beneath the waves.
What a relief it would be

to hear someone in the crew
cry out like a gull,
*Oh Captain, Captain!*
*Where are we going now?*

# Self-Improvement

Just before she flew off like a swan
to her wealthy parents' summer home,
Bruce's college girlfriend asked him
to improve his expertise at oral sex,
and offered him some technical advice:

Use nothing but his tonguetip
to flick the light switch in his room
on and off a hundred times a day
until he grew fluent at the nuances
of force and latitude.

Imagine him at practice every evening,
more inspired than he ever was at algebra,
beads of sweat sprouting on his brow,
thinking, *thirty-seven*, *thirty-eight*,
seeing, in the tunnel vision of his mind's eye,
the quadratic equation of her climax
yield to the logic
of his simple math.

Maybe he unscrewed
the bulb from his apartment ceiling
so that passersby would not believe
a giant firefly was pulsing
its electric abdomen in 13 B.

Maybe, as he stood
two inches from the wall,
in darkness, fogging the old plaster
with his breath, he visualized the future
as a mansion standing on the shore
that he was rowing to
with his tongue's exhausted oar.

Of course, the girlfriend dumped him:
met someone, après-ski, who,
using nothing but his nose
could identify the vintage of a Cabernet.

Sometimes we are asked
to get good at something we have
no talent for,
or we excel at something we will never
have the opportunity to prove.

Often we ask ourselves
to make absolute sense
out of what just happens,
and in this way, what we are practicing

is suffering,
which everybody practices,
but strangely few of us
grow graceful in.

The climaxes of suffering are complex,
costly, beautiful, but secret.
Bruce never played the light switch again.

So the avenues we walk down,
full of bodies wearing faces,
are full of hidden talent:
enough to make pianos moan,
sidewalks split,
streetlights deliriously flicker.

# Dickhead

To whomever taught me the word *dickhead*,
I owe a debt of thanks.
It gave me a way of being in the world of men
when I most needed one,

when I was pale and scrawny,
naked, goosefleshed
as a plucked chicken
in a supermarket cooler, a poor

forked thing stranded in the savage
universe of puberty, where wild
jockstraps flew across the steamy

skies of locker rooms,
and everybody fell down laughing
at jokes I didn't understand.

But *dickhead* was a word as dumb
and democratic as a hammer, an object
you could pick up in your hand,
and swing,

saying *dickhead* this and *dickhead* that,
a song that meant the world
was yours enough at least
to bang on like a garbage can,

and knowing it, and having that
beautiful ugliness always
cocked and loaded in my mind,
protected me and calmed me like a psalm.

Now I have myself become
a beautiful ugliness,

and my weakness is a fact
so well established that
it makes me calm,

and I am calm enough
to be grateful for the lives I
never have to live again;

but I remember all the bad old days
back in the world of men,
when everything was serious, mysterious, scary,
hairier and bigger than I was;

I recall when flesh
was what I hated, feared
and was excluded from:

Hardly knowing what I did,
or what would come of it,
I made a word my friend.

# Honda Pavarotti

I'm driving on the dark highway
when the opera singer on the radio
opens his great mouth
and the whole car plunges down the canyon of his throat.

So the night becomes an aria of stars and exit signs
as I steer through the galleries
of one dilated Italian syllable
after another. I love the passages in which

the rich flood of the baritone
strains out against the walls of the esophagus,
and I love the pauses
in which I hear the tenor's flesh labor to inhale

enough oxygen to take the next plummet
up into the chasm of the violins.
In part of the song, it sounds as if the singer
is being squeezed by an enormous pair of tongs

while his head and legs keep kicking.
In part of the song, it sounds as if he is
standing in the middle of a coliseum,
swinging a 300-pound lion by the tail,

the empire of gravity
conquered by the empire of aerodynamics,
the citadel of pride in flames
and the citizens of weakness
celebrating their defeat in chorus,

joy and suffering made one at last,
joined in everything a marriage is alleged to be,
though I know the woman he is singing for
is dead in a foreign language on the stage beside him,

though I know his chain mail is made of silver-painted plastic
and his mismanagement of money is legendary,
as I know I have squandered
most of my own life

in a haze of trivial distractions,
and that I will continue to waste it.
But wherever I was going, I don't care anymore,
because no place I could arrive at

is good enough for this, this thing made out of experience
but to which experience will never measure up.
And that dark and soaring fact
is enough to make me renounce the whole world

or fall in love with it forever.

# Game

On Thursday nights in spring,
the volleyball game starts up again,
though all the players on the team
have been replaced,
the way that all the cells have been replaced
in my sensitive fingertips,
which once explored the sweet,
unbelievably silk periphery
of Jennifer Martin,
who then surprised me
by one day simply vanishing.

Each time the ball is served to me,
I get a great constriction in my chest,
afraid that I might miss,
but the ball flies up and down,
and I survive. The energy
which gushes through all things,
looking for a place to stop, keeps going,
and Jennifer might be the name for all of this:

wild photons plunging into skin,
the wind-stirred clover in the unmown field,
the bees that sexually harass the flowers;
the tendril of the honeysuckle, reaching for the next
rung in its ascension
of the chain-link fence;
blue of Jennifer-inflected sky
and Jennifer alfalfa.

By the end of summer we all will be
a slightly darker shade of brown,
as if the skin remembered; a few more
tiny stretchmarks pleated at our eyes

as if we each were making a serious collection
of the kind of things that change
is gradually made of.

When my turn comes to serve,
I hold the white ball in my hand
as long as possible, letting it grow rounder,
making everybody wait until they get
impatient, pissed off, loud—

noticing the Jennifer-shaped cloud
that slides across the sun
above the field of sparkling Jennifer.
I hold it in my hand as long as possible,
though birds are speeding overhead
and the unmown field is foaming at the mouth with flowers.

# Medicine

The black hair of my Chinese doctor
gleams like combed ink
as he leans over his desk,
with quick pen strokes writing my prescription
in the lingo of the *I Ching*,
characters so intricate and strange,
the page looks like a street
lined with sampans and pagodas,
rickshaws gliding through the palace gates
bearing Szechuan takeout to the king.

Daydreaming comes easy to the ill:
slowed down to the speed of waiting rooms,
you learn to hang suspended in the wallpaper,
to drift among the magazines and plants,
feeling a strange love
for the time that might be killing you.

Two years ago, I was so infatuated
with my lady doctor, Linda,
I wanted to get better just to please her,
and yet to go on getting worse,
to keep her leaning toward me,
with her sea green eyes and stethoscope, asking
*Does that hurt?*

Does it hurt? Yes, it hurts
so sweet. It hurts exquisitely.
It hurts real good. I feel as if I read it
in some Bible for the ill,
that suffering itself is medicine
and to endure enough will cure you
of anything.

So I want more injury
and repair, an ulcer
and a migraine, please.
I want to suffer like my mother,

who said once, following a shot,
—her face joyful as the needle entered—
that she felt a train had been injected
straight into her vein. Day after day,
to see her sinking
through the layers of our care

was to learn something delicious
about weakness:
as if she had discovered
the train was bound somewhere;
as if the conductor
had told everyone on board
they never had to bear the weight
of being strong again.

# Beauty

When the medication she was taking
caused tiny vessels in her face to break,
leaving faint but permanent blue stitches in her cheeks,
my sister said she knew she would
never be beautiful again.

After all those years
of watching her reflection in the mirror,
sucking in her stomach and standing straight,
she said it was a relief,
being done with beauty,

but I could see her pause inside that moment
as the knowledge spread across her face
with a fine distress, sucking
the peach out of her lips,
making her cute nose seem, for the first time,
a little knobby.

I'm probably the only one in the whole world
who actually remembers the year in high school
she perfected the art
of being a dumb blond,

spending recess on the breezeway by the physics lab,
tossing her hair and laughing that canary trill
which was her specialty,

while some football player named Johnny
with a pained expression in his eyes
wrapped his thick finger over and over again
in the bedspring of one of those pale curls.

Or how she spent the next decade of her life
auditioning a series of tall men,

looking for just one with the kind
of attention span she could count on.

Then one day her time of prettiness
was over, done, finito,
and all those other beautiful women
in the magazines and on the streets
just kept on being beautiful
everywhere you looked,

walking in that kind of elegant, disinterested trance
in which you sense they always seem to have one hand
touching the secret place
that keeps their beauty safe,
inhaling and exhaling the perfume of it—

It was spring. Season when the young
buttercups and daisies climb up on the
mulched bodies of their forebears
to wave their flags in the parade.

My sister just stood still for thirty seconds,
amazed by what was happening,
then shrugged and tossed her shaggy head
as if she was throwing something out,

something she had carried a long ways,
but had no use for anymore,
now that it had no use for her.
That, too, was beautiful.

# Candlelight

Crossing the porch in the hazy dusk
to worship the moon rising
like a yellow filling-station sign
on the black horizon,

you feel the faint grit
of ants beneath your shoes,
but keep on walking
because in this world

you have to decide what
you're willing to kill.
Saving your marriage might mean
dinner for two

by candlelight on steak
raised on pasture
chopped out of rain forest
whose absence might mean

an atmospheric thinness
fifty years from now
above the vulnerable head
of your bald grandson on vacation

as the cells of his scalp
sautéed by solar radiation
break down like suspects
under questioning.

Still you slice
the sirloin into pieces
and feed each other
on silver forks

under the approving gaze
of a waiter
whose purchased attention
and French name

are a kind of candlelight themselves,
while in the background
the fingertips of the pianist
float over the tusks

of the slaughtered elephant
without a care,
as if the elephant
had granted its permission.

# Brave World

But what about the courage
of the cancer cell
that breaks out from the crowd
it has belonged to all its life

like a housewife erupting
from her line at the grocery store
because she just can't stand
the sameness anymore?

What about the virus that arrives
in town like a traveler
from somewhere faraway
with suitcases in hand,

who only wants a place
to stay, a chance to get ahead
in the land of opportunity,
but who smells bad,

talks funny, and reproduces fast?
What about the microbe that
hurls its tiny boat straight
into the rushing metabolic tide,

no less cunning and intrepid
than Odysseus; that gambles all
to found a city
on an unknown shore?

What about their bill of rights,
their access to a full-scale,
first-class destiny?
their chance to realize

maximum potential?—which, sure,
will come at the expense
of someone else, someone
who, from a certain point of view,

is a secondary character,
whose weeping is almost
too far off to hear,

a noise among the noises
coming from the shadows
of any brave new world.

# Lucky

If you are lucky in this life,
you will get to help your enemy
the way I got to help my mother
when she was weakened past the point of saying no.

Into the big enamel tub
half-filled with water
which I had made just right,
I lowered the childish skeleton
she had become.

Her eyelids fluttered as I soaped and rinsed
her belly and her chest,
the sorry ruin of her flanks
and the frayed gray cloud
between her legs.

Some nights, sitting by her bed
book open in my lap
while I listened to the air
move thickly in and out of her dark lungs,
my mind filled up with praise
as lush as music,

amazed at the symmetry and luck
that would offer me the chance to pay
my heavy debt of punishment and love
with love and punishment.

And once I held her dripping wet
in the uncomfortable air
between the wheelchair and the tub,
until she begged me like a child

to stop,
an act of cruelty which we both understood
was the ancient irresistible rejoicing
of power over weakness.

If you are lucky in this life,
you will get to raise the spoon
of pristine, frosty ice cream
to the trusting creature mouth
of your old enemy

because the tastebuds at least are not broken
because there is a bond between you
and sweet is sweet in any language.

# Benevolence

When my father dies and comes back as a dog,
I already know what his favorite sound will be:
the soft, almost inaudible gasp
as the rubber lips of the refrigerator door
unstick, followed by that arctic

exhalation of cold air;
then the cracking of the ice-cube tray above the sink
and the quiet *ching* the cubes make
when dropped into a glass.

Unable to pronounce the name of his favorite drink, or to express
his preference for single malt,
he will utter one sharp bark
and point the wet black arrow of his nose
imperatively up
at the bottle on the shelf,

then seat himself before me,
trembling, expectant, water pouring
down the long pink dangle of his tongue
as the memory of pleasure from his former life
shakes him like a tail.

What I'll remember as I tower over him,
holding a dripping, whiskey-flavored cube
above his open mouth,
relishing the power rushing through my veins
the way it rushed through his,

what I'll remember as I stand there
is the hundred clever tricks
I taught myself to please him,
and for how long I mistakenly believed
that it was love he held concealed in his closed hand.

# Auden

*Nicotine, caffeine, amphetamine*—these
were three of W.H. Auden's favorite words,
and he muttered them sometimes

as he shuffled through his Greenwich Village flat, at 2 A.M.
the hem of his tobacco-flecked old disreputable
robe dragging on the floor,

some long thought unwinding
through the mountains of his brain,
*choo choo* like a locomotive—no hill too

steep for his powerful vocabulary.
My friend who hates Auden says
he smotheringly reminds her

of one of those statues
seated in a granite lifeguard's chair
outside the city hall,

surrounded by the halo of the know-it-all,
but I think he had to stay up sometimes
three days and nights

to feel a feeling to completion,
watching the whole planet heat up
and then cool off,

feeling the warehouse of his skull
creak and groan in its accommodation,
wondering if he could get the whole

thing in: the armies swarming over nations
like ants on candy,
the million dialects of rain,

the dreams rising from the sleep of children
like air escaping from balloons.
All those years, he kept on growing

uglier and wiser,
moving farther back to get a better look
until one day he found himself entirely

outside the frame,
where he still resides—
a puff of smoke drifting from one ear,

teacup balanced on his knee,
another little pill, God bless the queen,
going down the hatch—

nicotine, caffeine, and amphetamine.

# Hearings

Autumn, and the trees decide again they don't
                                        need leaves.
Mothers add more blankets to the bed.
Yellow lights in windows of the junior high
mean that night school is back in session,
tired grown-ups sitting at the plastic desks,
learning to bisect the hypotenuse,
how to say *spreadsheet* in Japanese.

This week on the televised hearings,
we get to watch our congressmen
nervously pronounce the word *homosexual*
in public—the committee trying to determine
whether queers are good enough
                                        to pull the triggers
on machines designed to foreclose lives
contrary to the national well-being.

But the congressman can't
pull the trigger on his own tongue
to fire out the word without
tripping over it—fumbling, stumbling
into the ditch between *home* and *sexual*.

You might say his defense industry is troubled,
as if he had a subterranean suspicion
that to say it might mean, just a little,
to *become* it—
                which might be right,

since language uses us
the way that birds use sky,
the way that seeds and viruses

braid themselves into a mammal's fur
and hitchhike toward the future.

When you say a word,
you enter *its* vocabulary,
it's got your home address, your phone number
and weight—it won't forget,

—the way that parents, who finally
bring themselves to say *lesbian*,
enter, through that checkpoint,
the country where their daughter lives.

Tonight, all over Washington, senators in mirrors
will practice until they are as fluent
saying *homosexual*
as they already are at saying *Mr. President*,
and *first-strike option*.

Sometimes we think the truth
is the worst thing that could happen
but the truth is not the worst thing that could happen.

Now it is autumn and in stores
the turquoise wading pools
spangled with bright starfishes and shells
are stacked against the walls, on sale,

implying what was costly yesterday
is cheap today, and might be free tomorrow—
All our yearnings, all our fears:
so many seahorses,
galloping through bubbles.

# Lawrence

On two occasions in the past twelve months
I have failed, when someone at a party
spoke of him with a dismissive scorn,
to stand up for D.H. Lawrence,

a man who burned like an acetylene torch
from one end to the other of his life.
These individuals, whose relationship to literature
is approximately that of a tree shredder

to stands of old-growth forest,
these people leaned back in their chairs,
bellies full of dry white wine and the ova of some foreign fish,
and casually dropped his name

the way that pygmies with their little poison spears
strut around the carcass of a fallen elephant.
"O Elephant," they say,
"you are not so big and brave today!"

It's a bad day when people speak of their superiors
with a contempt they haven't earned,
and it's a sorry thing when certain other people

don't defend the great dead ones
who have opened up the world before them.
And though, in the catalogue of my betrayals,
this is a fairly minor entry,

I resolve, if the occasion should recur,
to uncheck my tongue and say, "I love the spectacle
of maggots condescending to a corpse,"
or, "You should be so lucky in your brainy, bloodless life

as to deserve to lift
just one of D.H. Lawrence's urine samples
to your arid psychobiographic
theory-tainted lips."

Or maybe I'll just take the shortcut
between the spirit and the flesh,
and punch someone in the face,
because human beings haven't come that far

in their effort to subdue the body,
and we still walk around like zombies
in our dying, burning world,
able to do little more

than fight, and fuck, and crow:
something Lawrence wrote about
in such a manner
as to make us seem magnificent.

# Fred Had Watched a Lot of *Kung Fu* Episodes

so when the policeman asked
to see his driver's license, he said,
*Does the wind need permission*

*from the hedgehog to blow*?
which resulted in a search of the car,
which miraculously yielded nothing

since Fred had swallowed all the mescaline already
and was just beginning to fall in love
with the bushy caterpillar eyebrows
of the officer in question.

In those days we could identify
the fingerprints on a guitar string
by the third note of the song
broadcast from the window of a passing car,

but we couldn't tell the difference
between a personal disaster
and "having an experience,"

so Fred thought being locked up for the night
was kind of fun,
with the graffiti on the drunk-tank wall
chattering in Mandarin
and the sentient cockroaches coming out to visit
in triplicate.

Back then it wasn't a question of pleasure or pain,
it wasn't a question of getting to the top
then trying not to fall at any cost.

It was a question of staying tuned in,
one episode at a time,
said Fred to himself

as he walked home the next morning
under the spreading lotus trees on Walnut Street,
feeling Oriental.

# Here in Berkeley

the jogger with the Rastafarian sweats
runs past the mechanic reading Marx on lunch break
with a sprout sandwich for a bookmark
as the sunlight through a bottle of Perrier
wobbles little rainbows on his knee.

On the corner, someone wearing I Ching earrings
is talking about personal space,
how she just can't take it anymore,
the way that Marcia's codependency
defeats her own empowerment.
"The whole seminar is out of whack," she says,
slapping a bouquet of daisies on her knee.

Close your eyes,
swing a baguette horizontally,
you'll hit someone with a Ph.D.
in sensitivity,
someone who,
if not a therapist himself,
will offer you the number of his therapist,

which—it may take you years
to figure out—is a hostile act on his part
designed to send you on a wild-goose chase
through the orchard of your childhood
to fetch the tarnished apple of your mother's love.

And if you don't like it,
there might be something
wrong with you. You might be so
reincarnationally headed
in the wrong direction,
that you can't hear the music hovering

above this zone of crystal vendors
and karmic mountaineers.

Now the traffic lights harmonically converge:
the traffic flows
past the bakeries and bookstores,
past the cappuccino depot and the acupuncture center.

No matter how you feel, you have to act
like you are very popular with yourself;
very relaxed and purposeful,
very unconfused
and not
like you are walking through the sunshine
singing
in chains.

# Muy Macho

I can't believe I'm sitting here
in this dark tavern,
listening to my old friend boast

about the size of his cock
and its long history,
as witnessed by the list of women

he now embarks upon, enumerating them
as a warrior might recite the deeds
accomplished by the family spear,

or like an old Homeric mariner might
go on about the nightspots
between Ithaca and Troy.

The bar tonight has the feeling
of a hideout deep inside the woods, a stronghold
full of beer and smoke,

the tidal undertow of baritones and jukebox
punctuated by the clean, authoritative smack
of pool balls from the back.

It's so primordial,
I feel my chest grow hairier
with every drink, and soon

I'm drunk enough to think
I'm also qualified to handle
any woman in the world.

You can talk about the march
of evolutionary change,
you can talk about how far we've climbed

up that staircase lined with self-help books
and sensitivity exams,
but my friend and I,

we're no different from any pair
of good old boy Neanderthals
crouching by their fire

a million years ago,
showing off their scars and belching
as they scratch their heavy, king-size balls.

I know that we are just an itchy spot
in the middle of the back
of that great hairy beast, The Truth;

I know that every word we say is probably a stone
someone else will someday have to
kick aside,

—still, part of me feels privileged,
belonging to this tribe of predators,
this club of deep-voiced woman-fuckers

to which I never thought
I ever would belong;
part of me is more than willing to be wrong

to remain inside the circle of this
conversation,
—to hear the details, one more time,

of how she took her shirt off, smiled,
and then they did it on the floor.
Even if the roof were falling in,

even if the whole world splintered and caught fire,
I would continue sitting here, I think,
entranced—implicated, cursed,

historically entwined—
another little dinosaur
stretching up its neck and head

to catch the last sweet drop of drunken warmth
coming from that ancient, fading sun.
We can't pull ourselves apart from it.

We don't really believe
there is another one.

# Lie Down with a Man

In those days I thought I had to
do everything I was afraid of,
so I lay down with a man.

It was one item on a list—
sleeping in the graveyard, under the full moon,
not looking away from the burned girl's stricken face,
strapping myself into the catapult
of some electric blue pill.

It was the seventies, a whole generation of us
was more than willing to chainsaw through
the branch that we were sitting on
to see what falling felt like—*bump bump bump.*

Knowing the worst about yourself
seemed like self-improvement then,
and suffering was adventure.

So I lay down with a man,
which I really don't remember
except that it was humorless.

Curtains fluttered in the breeze
from the radio's black grill. Van Morrison
filled up the room like astral aftershave.

I lay my mass of delusions
next to his mass of delusions
in a dark room where I struggled
with the old adversary, myself

—in the form, this time, of a body—
someplace between heaven and earth,
two things I was afraid of.

# The Replacement

And across the country I know
they are replacing my brother's brain
with the brain of a man:

one gesture, one word, one neuron at a time
with surgical precision
they are teaching him to hook his thumbs
into his belt, to iron his mouth as flat
as the horizon, and make his eyes
reflective as a piece of tin.

It is a kind of cooking
the male child undergoes:
to toughen him, he is dipped repeatedly
in insult—*peckerwood, shitbag, faggot,
pussy, dicksucker*—until spear points
will break against his epidermis,
until he is impossible to disappoint.

Then he walks out into the street
ready for a game of corporate poker
with a hard-on for the Dow-Jones
like this hormonal language I am
flexing like a bicep
to show who's boss.

But I'm not the boss.
And there is nothing I can do to stop it,
and would I if I could?
What else is there for him to be
except a man?
If they fail,
he stumbles through his life

like an untied shoe.
If they succeed, he may become
something even I can't love.

Already the photograph I have of him
is out of date
but in it he is standing by the pool
without a shirt: too young, too white, too weak,
with feelings he is too inept to hide
splashed all over his face—

goofy, proud, shy,
he's smiling at the camera
as if he were under the illusion
that someone loved him so well
they would not ever ever ever
turn him over to the world.

# Research

That summer, Vietnam was heating up,
and at the press conferences, our Texas president
drawled each syllable
with such a Southern slowness

it felt like he was raising up a ladle
from a pot of soup
and tasting it to see if it was done.

*Life* magazine published a special issue
called *The Mind-Body Split*
about a recently discovered fracture
in the human condition,

but what I remember better is
the research all the rest of us were doing
in the densely populated dark
behind the old Safari Bar,

where the drumbeat of the band thudded
through the plywood walls
out into the jungle of the parking lot,
and the mosquitos came in droves to feast

on car after car of teenage bodies
making out in an intoxicated haze
of sweat and skin.

And how the tough guys, the really tough ones,
after they got drunk enough,
would leave their girls
and gather in a circle to perform

the trick of placing a lit cigarette
in the crook of their own arms,

then crushing it out
while staring into their best friend's eyes
and screaming the words of the latest song
over the perfume of burning flesh.

# Why We Went and What We Found

We will find the grail.
We will gallop our horses all night
and at dawn, descend from twisted mountain roads
to the plaza of a town without a name.
At the bronze hour when the sun
melts on the horizon like an old doubloon,
we will sail our ship into the harbor,
—salt crusted in our beards, trembling from years of motion
without maps or compasses; a little daffy from the velvet
sibilance of waves.
                          The prow will touch the stone wharf
without a sound, the nightingales
will trill, the dead oak shaft of the
*No Trespassing* sign will blossom morning glories.
The mute beggar by the church will launch into an aria
in perfect, unaccented Italian

and we will hoist the bucket from the courtyard well
on its frayed rope
and drink the sacred water
as the horses nicker
and the almond trees
drop their white petals of applause.
If the order comes to burn the bridges,
we will burn the bridges.
If the order comes to cast ourselves into the sea,
                                              we jump.

When we wake up in the morning, we will be ourselves again,
and begin our post-grail lives.
We will return to our people
who eat mud and say that it is good,

and we will eat the mud with them and say that it is good.
But it will never taste the same to us
in our post-grail existence.

Something will be missing we can't say.
No one will understand the *Ph.G.* we sign after our names,
or why we press our faces
deep into the artificial flowers,
half-hoping to be stung by bees.
Why we always go astray inside the glittering maze
of the department store,
and always end up at the perfume counter, wearing
scents called *Shangri-La, Obsession, Holy Night*,

finding none of them quite right,
none of them equal to a blow on the head
with a silver mace, a word whispered in a dream
like a gold key slid across a grate.

They won't understand, and we won't remember,
but we will never again be sad — never sad again! —
Or rather, never sad in the same way.

*for Dean Young*

# Just Spring

The teenage boys who broke into
Our Lady of the Sacred Heart
to graffiti their new vocabulary
of swear words on the white white walls
were attracted enough by the church, at least,
to vandalize it.

They broke the virgin's plaster nose
with baseball bats
and marked her private parts with orange spray paint
because they loved their mothers so much
it was killing them,

but they left the gaunt, adolescent torso of Jesus
hanging on the wall, untouched
because they didn't recognize themselves.

Or maybe it's just Spring,
which drives more than birds and flowers crazy.

*Desire*, someone says,
polishing his turbo-charged Camaro in the drive,
running his hand over its curves,

*it's a bitch.*
The blurred blue letters of the name *Diane*
scorched into his forearm
record a season in his life
he probably regrets,

but desire, if you don't let it out, everybody knows
backs up and poisons you inside
like old sap clogged inside a tree,

or like the hard line of JoAnn's mouth
when she said,
speaking of her first and recently demolished marriage,
*Never Again,*

gripping the steering wheel with both hands
and jamming the gas pedal
straight down into the floor,

though she still wants to be followed, pulled over,
taken out and carried off into the heavenly tall grass
of heterosexual imagination,

and kissed all over her thirty-nine-year-old body
until, like Spring,
she comes and comes and comes.
Suffering Mother of God. Sweet Jesus.

# Grammar

Maxine, back from a weekend with her boyfriend,
smiles like a big cat and says
that she's a conjugated verb.
She's been doing the direct object
with a second person pronoun named Phil,
and when she walks into the room,
everybody turns:

some kind of light is coming from her head.
Even the geraniums look curious,
and the bees, if they were here, would buzz
suspiciously around her hair, looking
for the door in her corona.
We're all attracted to the perfume
of fermenting joy,

we've all tried to start a fire,
and one day maybe it will blaze up on its own.
In the meantime, she is the one today among us
most able to bear the idea of her own beauty,
and when we see it, what we do is natural:
we take our burned hands
out of our pockets,
and clap.

# From This Height

Cold wind comes out of the white hills
and rubs itself against the walls of the condominium
with an esophogeal vowel sound,
and a loneliness creeps
into the conversation by the hot tub.

We don't deserve pleasure
just as we don't deserve pain,
but it's pure sorcery the way the feathers of warm mist
keep rising from the surface of the water
to wrap themselves around a sculpted
clavicle or wrist.

It's not just that we are on
the eighth story of the world
looking out through glass and steel
with a clarity of vision
in which imported coffee and
a knowledge of French painting

                              are combined,

but that we are atop a pyramid
of all the facts that make this possible:
the furnace that heats the water,
the truck that hauled the fuel,
the artery of highway
blasted through the mountains,

the heart attack of the previous owner,
the history of Western medicine
that failed to save him,
the successful development of tourism,
the snow white lotions that counteract the chemistry
of chlorine upon skin—our skin.

Down inside history's body,
the slaves are still singing in the dark;
the roads continue to be built;
the wind blows and the building grips itself
in anticipation of the next strong gust.

So an enormous act of forgetting is required
simply to kiss someone
or to open your mouth
for the fork of high-calorie paté
someone is raising to your lips,

which, considering the price,
it would be a sin
not to enjoy.

# Mission

When I remember Susan, she is always
kneeling over me, looking down,
her green, nineteen-year-old eyes
wide open & half blind
as the flush spreads
between the freckles on her high cheekbones.
Her lips turn scarlet as I put her fingers in my mouth
and our hips are locked into each other
like the guidance systems of two rockets
whose only mission at this moment
is to make the other blow up first.

This time it's her, and her face
takes on the troubled, *is-this-pain-
or-pleasure?* look that people wear
when the train they're waiting for
comes through the station wall in flames,
the long legs of the water tower break
and desire drowns in its own destination.

We don't notice we are young,
or that she is going to have four kids
with an Italian oilman,
or that I'll get sick and stay that way
for years, caught in my condition
like a fly in glue.

We won't know each other then.
Right now, all systems are go, everything
exactly where it needs to be.
Except her pale breasts are hanging
where I can't quite reach them
with my breathless mouth.

# Cry Me a River

Once upon a time there were five brothers.
One could hear an acorn drop a hundred miles away.
The second could understand the speech of animals.
Another could make his legs grow very long.
The fourth had read every book ever written,
and could remember every word.
The last could weep to flood the world.

Let us say they were Chinese.
And the fourth one ran through the library of his mind
and said, "The sublateral equation of 100 kilotons of hydrophobia
in the second week of April equals precisely 4,000 loaves of bread
and 15 cups of sugar."
And that was the right answer.

The king's scientists were dazzled.
And then of course grew jealous.
I can almost remember the day
my heart stopped feeling anything.
I stood up from my body at the dinner table
and walked away from that strange silence
like a man who leaves his deserted smoking village
to wander through the world forevermore.

But the brothers kept getting into trouble.
And the first brother eavesdropped on the conversation
of two mice who lived beneath the palace floor,
and he repeated what he heard to Brother Number Three,
who could translate mouse dialect,
and *he* said, "The king's feet are hurting him tonight
so he is going to march into Fredonia tomorrow
and burn the countryside."

Why are they brothers and not sisters?
All this happened long ago, so we can't ask.
Of childhood, I have just the faintest recollection.
It's like the black-and-white footage of a distant place
on a television with the sound turned off.

And the swift brother ran like the west wind on amphetamines
and fetched a bucketful of snow from the mountaintop
and brought it to the king, who put his feet in.
And the countryside was peaceful for a while.

Has anyone had a normal life?
That we could use as reference?
Trying to imagine that is like trying to imagine
what it would be like to be smarter than you are.

Then something else happened—the queen
was kidnapped by a band of traveling alcoholics.
And the king sent for the five brothers,
to bring their skills, posthaste.

And the fifth brother—whose job it was
to have feelings for the rest of them—said,
"I have four brothers but I am lonely."

And the smart brother said, "My calculations show
that the king will never be satisfied."

And the second brother and the third
said that they were tired of being exceptional.
None of them had slept in years.

And the first brother, who had been listening closely,
said, "I can hear the future coming toward us,
and I think that where we come from
doesn't matter anymore."

And the ugly brother said—he was ugly
as well as emotional—"I will teach you how to cry."
And his tears fell down in such profusion

they formed a river of considerable size.
And all the boys fell in, got wet,
and felt much better afterward.

They named the river *Evangeline*, in honor of the queen,
who was never saved, whom they praised whenever
they went fishing, which was all the time.
And that was the world's first Country-Western song.

# Memory As a Hearing Aid

Somewhere, someone is asking a question,
and I stand squinting at the classroom
with one hand cupped behind my ear,
trying to figure out where that voice is coming from.

I might be already an old man,
attempting to recall the night
his hearing got misplaced,
front-row-center at a battle of the bands,

where a lot of leather-clad, second-rate musicians,
amped up to dinosaur proportions,
test drove their equipment through our ears.
Each time the drummer threw a tantrum,

the guitarist whirled and sprayed us with machine-gun riffs,
as if they wished that they could knock us
quite literally dead.
We called that fun in 1970,

when we weren't sure our lives were worth surviving.
I'm here to tell you that they were,
and many of us did, despite ourselves,
though the road from there to here

is paved with dead brain cells,
parents shocked to silence,
and squad cars painting the whole neighborhood
the quaking tint and texture of red jelly.

Friends, we should have postmarks on our foreheads
to show where we have been;
we should have pointed ears, or polka-dotted skin
to show what we were thinking

when we hot-rodded over God's front lawn,
and Death kept blinking.
But here I stand, an average-looking man
staring at a room

where someone blond in braids
with a beautiful belief in answers
is still asking questions.

Through the silence in my dead ear,
I can almost hear the future whisper
to the past: it says that this is not a test
and everybody passes.

# Arrows

When a beautiful woman wakes up,
she checks to see if her beauty is still there.
When a sick person wakes up,
he checks to see if he continues to be sick.

He takes the first pills in a thirty-pill day,
looks out the window at a sky
where a time-release sun is crawling
through the milky X ray of a cloud.

✦ ✦ ✦ ✦ ✦

I sing the body like a burnt-out fuse box,
the wires crossed, the panel lit
by red malfunction lights, the pistons firing
out of sequence,
the warning sirens blatting in the empty halls,

and the hero is trapped in a traffic jam,
the message doesn't reach its destination,
the angel falls down into the body of a dog
and is speechless,

tearing at itself with fast white teeth;
and the consciousness twists evasively,
like a sheet of paper,
        traveled by blue tongues of flame.

✦ ✦ ✦ ✦ ✦

In the famous painting, the saint
looks steadfastly heavenward,
            away from the physical indignity below,

the fascinating spectacle
   of his own body
             bristling with arrows;
he looks up
as if he were already adamantly elsewhere,
   exerting that power of denial
       the soul is famous for,
that ability to say, "None of this is real:

Nothing that happened here on earth
and who I thought I was,
and nothing that I did or that was done to me,
was ever real."

# Embarrassment

The high school Latin teacher
who has to tell his pretty student
that the most accurate translation
of the noun in her Catullus ode
is *blowjob*
blushes,

though the blood that rushes
through the capillaries of his cheeks
is exactly the same force of nature
Catullus often praised
as the inspiration
of the cock.

Ask God which he prefers:
doing,
or watching?
He'll just shrug and give
that lazy, crooked smile
that could mean enlightenment
or indigestion,
or something in between,

like we are, trying:
one person eating oatmeal
and another, wanting nothing more
than to be the spoon,

and hiding it.

# The Confessional Mode

"I wish somebody would take a razor
and just slit my throat,"
my mother often used to say
at that lovely time of evening

when the stars gleamed like spangles on a corset
wrapped around the broad, ungirlish waist of Earth.
"Put a bag over my head, pretty please,
and let me blow my brains out in the sink."

The mouth is such a terrible instrument,
such a bloody harmonica,
wailing its complaints,
but it's the great insulters we remember,

the ones with a vocabulary
of cancer and barbed wire.
"I'm the fucking Jew here," she would announce,

setting down the dinner plates, smiling like a woman
invited to consume a meal of broken teeth,
and everyone would sigh and shiver
over their spaghetti, and wait for that particular

Russian novel to be over.
What strange appetites we have
that make us rewind time and summon up
the landscapes of our pain

long after the lips have been unleashed
from their humiliated smiles,
and the silverware gone to the graveyard
for old forks and knives.

Yet some craving draws me backward
and the words for telling it

march out of my mouth with a pleasure
that is almost biological,

as if the telling were a sort of sweet revenge,
though I have noticed also how
each telling renders me
a little bit more ruthless, old

and capable of saying anything.

# Adam and Eve

I wanted to punch her right in the mouth and that's the truth.

After all, we had gotten from the station of the flickering glances
to the station of the hungry mouths,
from the shoreline of skirts and faded jeans
to the ocean of unencumbered skin,
from the perilous mountaintop of the apartment steps
to the sanctified valley of the bed—

the candle fluttering upon the dresser top, its little yellow blade
sending up its whiff of waxy smoke,
and I could smell her readiness
like a dank cloud above a field,

when at the crucial moment, the all-important moment,
the moment standing at attention,

she held her milk white hand agitatedly
over the entrance to her body and said *No*,

and my brain burst into flame.

If I couldn't sink myself in her like a dark spur
or dissolve into her like a clod thrown in a river,

can I go all the way in the saying, and say
I wanted to punch her right in the face?
Am I allowed to say that,
that I wanted to punch her right in her soft face?

Or is the saying just another instance of rapaciousness,
just another way of doing what I wanted then,
by saying it?

Is a man just an animal, and is a woman not an animal?
Is the name of the animal power?
Is it true that the man wishes to see the woman
hurt with her own pleasure

and the woman wishes to see the expression on the man's face
of someone falling from great height,
that the woman thrills with the power of her weakness
and the man is astonished by the weakness of his power?

Is the sexual chase a hunt where the animal inside
drags the human down
into a jungle made of vowels,
hormonal undergrowth of sweat and hair,

or is this an obsolete idea
lodged like a fossil
in the brain of the ape
who lives inside the man?

Can the fossil be surgically removed
or dissolved, or redesigned
so the man can be a human being, like a woman?

Does the woman see the man as a house
where she might live in safety,
and does the man see the woman as a door
through which he might escape
the hated prison of himself,

and when the door is locked,
does he hate the door instead?
Does he learn to hate all doors?

I've seen rain turn into snow then back to rain,
and I've seen making love turn into fucking
then back to making love,
and no one covered up their faces out of shame,
no one rose and walked into the lonely maw of night.

But where was there, in fact, to go?
Are some things better left unsaid?
Shall I tell you her name?
Can I say it again,
that I wanted to punch her right in the face?

Until we say the truth, there can be no tenderness.
As long as there is desire, we will not be safe.

# Are You Experienced?

While Jimi Hendrix played "Purple Haze" onstage,
scaling his guitar like a black cat
up a high-voltage, psychedelic fence,

I was in the parking lot of the rock festival,
trying to get away from the noise and
looking for my car because

I wanted to have something familiar
to throw up next to. The haze I was in
was actually ultraviolet, the murky lavender

of the pills I had swallowed
several hundred years before,
pills that had answered so many of my questions,

they might as well have been guided tours
of miniature castles and museums,
microscopic Sistine Chapels

with room for everyone inside.
—But now something was backfiring,
and I was out on the perimeter of history,

gagging at the volume of raw data,
unable to recall the kind and color
of the car I owned,

and unable to guess, as I studied
the fresco of vomit on concrete,
that one day this moment

cleaned up and polished
would itself become
a kind of credential.

# Ecology

Mike moved to the city
to begin his life as an adult
and to immerse himself in the cultural milieu

but he wound up being one of those fishes
employed to use their mouths
to vacuum the glass walls of the aquarium,

—hanging around the edges of the party,
fluttering his gills,
trying to get closer to the center of the room

where the big fish flash
their golden fins expansively. . . .
And isn't that the way it goes

when you traffic with power?
There's always someone
with a bigger tail,

more talent, better clothes,
someone whose blue blood
and collegiate chin

or low-cut dress
and cappuccino skin
have something you suspect

to do with their success.
Thus it was in the tiled courts
of the Roman kings:

Flaccus peering enviously
over Tiberion's shoulder
to where Chloe is

dripping her sweet vowels
like a trickle of honey
into the princeling's ear.

The world has always
moved that way,
small fry darting

on the edges of the big
ones ploughing forward,
and you live on what they spill

from the corners of their mouths,
scraps of money and prestige
floating in their wake.
Curse if you want,

but it's just ecology at work,
and you continue
doing what you think is necessary

on a level that is simple, automatic, blessed
in a way that you
no longer see,

even as you wiggle your fins
and lash your tail
with all the skill that you've acquired

to hold your place
among the others,
like miserable Mike, to whom

everything he has
looks like just a snack.
Mike, when you were a kid

you used to have
some imagination.
Now, how will you imagine

your way out of this?

# Totally

I'm raking leaves and singing in my off-key voice
a mangled version of Madonna's "Like a Virgin,"
a song I thought I hated;

that's how it goes when your head and heart
are in different time zones—
you often don't find out till tomorrow
what you felt today.

I know I do not understand the principles
of leaf removal; I pile them up
in glowing heaps of cadmium and orange,

but I identify so much more
with the entropic gusts of wind
that knock them all apart again.
Is it natural to be scattered?

When I look into the sky I am often dreaming
of a television program that I saw some months ago;
when I walk into a dinner party

I am thinking of the book I mean to read
when I get home—you might say
my here is disconnected from my now,
so never am I entirely anywhere,

or anyone. But I won't speak cruelly
of myself: this dividedness is just what
makes our species great: possible for Darwin

to figure out his theory of selection
while playing five-card stud,
for surgeon Keats to find a perfect rhyme

wrist-deep in the disorder
of an open abdomen.

For example, it is autumn here.
The defoliated trees look frightened
at the edge of town,

as if the train they missed
had taken all their clothes.
The whole world in unison is turning
toward a zone of nakedness and cold.

But me, I have this strange conviction
that I am going to be born.

TONY HOAGLAND is the author of three collections of poems, most recently *What Narcissism Means to Me* and a collection of essays, *Real Sofistikashun. Donkey Gospel* is the winner of the James Laughlin Award of The Academy of American Poets. Hoagland teaches at the University of Houston.

This book was designed by Will Powers. It is set in Calisto type by Stanton Publication Services, Inc., and the book was manufactured by Versa Press on acid-free paper.